RANJOT SINGH CHAHAL

The Skill Master's Guide

How to Improve Skills from the Beginning

Contents

Introduction

Skill development is crucial for personal and professional growth in today's rapidly changing world. It refers to the process of acquiring and honing various abilities knowledge and competencies that enable individuals to perform tasks effectively and efficiently. Whether in the workplace or in everyday life skill development plays a significant role in achieving success and adapting to evolving circumstances.

Here are some key reasons why skill development is important:

1. Enhances Employability: In a highly competitive job market possessing relevant skills can give individuals a competitive edge. Employers seek candidates who possess a diverse range of skills and are adaptable to new challenges. By continually developing and upgrading their skills individuals can increase their employability and improve their chances of landing their desired jobs.

2. Promotes Career Advancement: Skill development is closely linked to career progression. By continuously enhancing their skills individuals can expand their knowledge base and stay up-to-date with industry trends. This not only helps them

contribute more effectively to their current roles but also increases their chances of promotion and opens doors for new career opportunities.

3. Fosters Personal Growth: Engaging in skill development activities can have a positive impact on personal growth. Learning new skills enhances cognitive abilities problem-solving skills and critical thinking. It broadens perspectives encourages personal creativity and boosts self-confidence. This in turn leads to personal satisfaction and a sense of accomplishment.

4. Adapts to Changing Workforce Needs: The workforce landscape is constantly evolving due to technological advancements and changing market demands. Skill development enables individuals to keep up with these changes and remain relevant. By continuously upgrading their skills individuals can adapt to emerging trends embrace new technologies and stay ahead of the curve. This flexibility and adaptability are crucial for long-term career success.

5. Increases Productivity and Efficiency: Possessing the right skills helps individuals work smarter not harder. Skill development leads to improved efficiency as individuals become proficient in their tasks and are equipped to handle challenges effectively. By mastering specific skills individuals can accomplish work more efficiently meet deadlines and produce high-quality outputs. This ultimately translates into increased productivity which benefits both individuals and organizations.

6. Encourages Innovation and Creativity: Skill development fosters a culture of innovation and creativity. As individuals

explore new skills and knowledge they are better equipped to generate fresh ideas and solutions. This leads to improved problem-solving abilities a more creative approach to tasks and the ability to think outside the box. Nurturing these skills not only benefits individual growth but also contributes to organizational success and competitiveness.

7. Enhances Personal and Professional Networks: Skill development often involves networking and collaboration with others. By engaging in training programs workshops and skill-building activities individuals have the opportunity to connect with like-minded people and experts in their field. Building a strong professional network can open doors to new opportunities collaborations and mentorship which further supports career growth.

In conclusion skill development is essential for personal and professional success. It empowers individuals to adapt to changing circumstances enhances employability fosters personal growth increases productivity and promotes innovation and creativity. By investing time and effort in developing new skills and upgrading existing ones individuals can stay competitive in the ever-evolving global landscape.

Setting Goals and Commitment:

Setting goals is an integral part of achieving success in any area of life including learning. When it comes to learning setting clear and specific goals is essential to provide direction and keep oneself motivated throughout the learning process. Here are some key steps to set effective learning goals:

1. Identify your purpose: Start by understanding why you want to learn a particular subject or skill. Determine whether it's for personal growth career advancement or any other purpose. This will give you a sense of direction and help you set appropriate goals.

2. Make your goals specific and measurable: Clearly define what you want to achieve in terms of knowledge skills or outcomes. For example instead of setting a vague goal like "I want to learn programming set a specific goal like "I want to learn Python programming language and build a basic web application within six months."

3. Break down your goals: Divide your goals into smaller manageable tasks or milestones. This will make them less overwhelming and easier to track progress. Create a timeline or action plan with deadlines for each milestone.

4. Set realistic yet challenging goals: Make sure your goals are attainable within your current capabilities and resources. At the same time include some level of challenge to push yourself out of your comfort zone and promote continuous growth.

5. Write down your goals: Document your goals on paper or electronically. This creates a sense of commitment and makes them more concrete. Review and revise your goals periodically to ensure they are still aligned with your learning journey.

Commitment is vital for achieving your learning goals. Here are some strategies to enhance commitment:

1. Develop a growth mindset: Embrace the belief that your abilities can be improved through effort and learning. Recognize that challenges and setbacks are part of the learning process rather than viewing them as failures.

2. Find your motivation: Understand what drives you to learn and stay committed. It could be intrinsic motivation such as personal interest or passion for the subject or extrinsic motivation such as career advancement or the desire to impress others.

3. Create a supportive environment: Surround yourself with like-minded individuals mentors or learning communities that can offer support encouragement and accountability. Engage in discussions share progress and seek feedback to stay motivated.

4. Break tasks into smaller manageable chunks: Large and complex tasks can be overwhelming leading to a loss of motivation. Breaking them down into smaller actionable steps makes them more manageable and helps maintain momentum.

5. Track your progress: Regularly monitor and evaluate your progress to stay motivated and make necessary adjustments. This can be done through self-reflection keeping a journal or using digital tools that measure and visualize progress.

Understanding the Learning Process:

Understanding the learning process can greatly optimize your learning experience and help you become a more effective learner. Here's a breakdown of the key stages involved:

1. Pre-learning stage: This stage involves preparing yourself mentally and physically before engaging in the learning process. It includes setting goals gathering necessary resources creating a conducive learning environment and building a positive mindset.

2. Acquisition stage: In this stage you actively engage with the learning materials whether it's reading books watching lectures participating in classes or using interactive online platforms. This stage focuses on acquiring new information concepts and skills.

3. Practice stage: Practice is crucial for mastery. In this stage you apply and reinforce what you have learned through various activities exercises problem-solving and real-world applications. Regular practice enhances retention and helps transfer knowledge to long-term memory.

4. Feedback and evaluation stage: This stage involves seeking feedback either from self-assessment or external sources like teachers mentors or peers. Feedback helps identify strengths areas for improvement and provides guidance on how to adjust your learning strategies.

5. Reflection and consolidation stage: Reflection is an essential part of the learning process. It allows you to absorb and make meaning of what you have learned connect new knowledge with prior knowledge and solidify your understanding. Take time to

reflect on what worked well what challenges you faced and how to improve future learning experiences.

6. Transfer and application stage: This stage focuses on applying what you have learned in new contexts or real-life situations. Transfer of learning occurs when knowledge and skills are effectively applied beyond the original learning context. Actively seek opportunities to apply your learning to reinforce and deepen your understanding.

Understanding the learning process helps you navigate through each stage efficiently adapt your learning strategies and make continuous improvement. By recognizing the stages and employing effective learning techniques you can make the most of your learning journey.

Chapter 1: The Mindset for Mastery

In order to achieve mastery in any area of life it is essential to develop the right mindset. The mindset for mastery involves adopting certain attitudes beliefs and perspectives that enable individuals to overcome challenges persist in the face of obstacles and continually grow and improve. This chapter will delve into the key elements of the mindset for mastery and provide practical strategies for cultivating it.

1. Embrace a Growth Mindset: One of the fundamental aspects of the mindset for mastery is having a growth mindset. Psychologist Carol S. Dweck coined this term which refers to the belief that abilities and intelligence can be developed through dedication hard work and perseverance. People with a growth mindset view challenges as opportunities for growth welcome feedback as a means to learn and improve and see failures as stepping stones on the path to success. By adopting a growth mindset individuals are more likely to embrace challenges set meaningful goals and put in the necessary effort to achieve mastery.

2. Develop Resilience: Resilience is another crucial component of the mindset for mastery. It involves the ability to bounce back from setbacks adapt to changing circumstances and stay focused and determined in the face of adversity. Resilient individuals understand that setbacks and failures are part of the learning process and view them as opportunities for growth. They recognize that setbacks do not define them but rather serve as valuable feedback for improvement. To develop resilience it is important to practice self-care cultivate a positive support system and engage in activities that build mental and emotional strength.

3. Foster a Passion for Learning: Those who have achieved mastery in their fields are often deeply passionate about what they do. They have a genuine curiosity and hunger for knowledge constantly seeking new information and understanding. This passion for learning fuels their motivation drives them to explore new possibilities and helps them stay committed to their goals. To foster a passion for learning it is important to explore different subjects find what genuinely interests you and engage in continuous learning through reading attending workshops or seeking out mentors.

4. Cultivate Discipline and Consistency: Mastery requires discipline and consistent effort over time. It is not achieved overnight but rather through deliberate practice and sustained focus. Building a routine setting specific goals and breaking them down into manageable tasks are essential for cultivating discipline and consistency. It is also important to hold oneself accountable and have a strong work ethic. By showing up consistently and putting in the necessary work individuals can

make steady progress towards mastery.

5. Embrace a Long-Term Perspective: Mastery is a journey that requires patience and a long-term perspective. It is not about immediate gratification or quick fixes but rather about committing to continuous learning and improvement over time. Individuals with the mindset for mastery understand that setbacks and temporary failures are part of the process and do not deter them from their ultimate goals. By keeping their eyes on the bigger picture and understanding that mastery is a lifelong pursuit they are able to persevere and maintain their motivation even during challenging times.

Developing a Growth Mindset:

Developing a growth mindset involves cultivating a belief that your abilities and intelligence can be improved with effort practice and learning. This mindset focuses on embracing challenges persisting through obstacles and seeking opportunities for personal growth and development. Here are some key aspects of developing a growth mindset:

1. Understand the power of effort: A growth mindset recognizes that talent and innate abilities are just starting points and success comes through effort perseverance and continuous learning. It means understanding that you can improve and expand your skills and knowledge through dedication and hard work.

2. Embrace challenges: Instead of shying away from difficult tasks a growth mindset encourages you to see challenges as op-

portunities for growth and learning. By approaching challenges with a positive attitude and a willingness to learn from mistakes you can overcome obstacles and reach new levels of success.

3. Learn from failure: Failure is seen as a stepping stone to success rather than a sign of personal inadequacy. Adopting a growth mindset means seeing failures as valuable learning experiences that can help you improve and develop new strategies. It involves analyzing setbacks learning from them and using the lessons to better yourself.

Overcoming Fear of Failure:

Fear of failure can often hold us back from taking risks pursuing goals and embracing new opportunities. However overcoming this fear is essential for personal growth and success. Here are some strategies to help overcome the fear of failure:

1. Recognize the potential for growth: Understand that failure is not the end but rather a necessary part of the learning process. Reframe failure as an opportunity for growth and improvement rather than a personal flaw or permanent setback.

2. Take small steps: Start by taking small manageable risks and gradually push your boundaries. Each small success will build confidence and resilience making it easier to tackle larger challenges.

3. Shift your mindset: Cultivate a positive and optimistic mindset that views failure as a normal part of the journey towards success. Focus on the lessons learned and the personal

growth gained from each experience regardless of the outcome.

4. Set realistic expectations: Unrealistic expectations can contribute to fear of failure. Set goals that are challenging but attainable and remember that setbacks and mistakes are inevitable on the path to success.

Embracing Challenges and Persistence:

Embracing challenges and persisting through difficulties is crucial for personal growth and achieving long-term success. Here are some ways to embrace challenges and cultivate persistence:

1. Adopt a growth mindset: Embracing challenges starts by believing in your ability to learn grow and overcome obstacles. A growth mindset allows you to view challenges as opportunities for development rather than threats to your abilities.

2. Set clear goals: Clearly define your goals and break them down into smaller manageable steps. This way challenges become more approachable and less overwhelming.

3. Develop resilience: Build resilience by learning from failures bouncing back from setbacks and maintaining a positive attitude. Embrace challenges as opportunities for personal growth and develop strategies to overcome obstacles.

4. Seek support: Surround yourself with a supportive network of friends mentors or colleagues who can provide encouragement guidance and accountability. Having a support system can boost your confidence and help you stay motivated when faced with

challenges.

5. Celebrate progress: Acknowledge and celebrate your achievements along the way. Recognize the efforts and progress you've made even if you haven't reached your ultimate goal yet. This will fuel your motivation and encourage you to persist in the face of challenges.

Overall developing a growth mindset overcoming the fear of failure and embracing challenges with persistence are essential ingredients for personal growth success and fulfillment in various aspects of life. By adopting and nurturing these attitudes and behaviors you can unlock your full potential and achieve your goals.

Chapter 2: Identifying Your Strengths and Weaknesses

Introduction:

Identifying your strengths and weaknesses is a crucial step in personal and professional development. By understanding your strengths you can leverage them to achieve success and find fulfillment. On the other hand recognizing your weaknesses allows you to work on improving or finding ways to compensate for them. In this chapter we will explore different methods and strategies to identify your strengths and weaknesses.

1. Self-Reflection:

One of the first steps in identifying your strengths and weaknesses is self-reflection. Take the time to introspect and analyze your skills qualities and experiences. Consider both your personal and professional life as strengths and weaknesses can manifest in various areas.

a) Strengths: Think about the tasks or activities that come naturally to you or that you excel in. Identify the skills you possess such as communication problem-solving creativity leadership or technical expertise. Look back at your achievements and note the skills or qualities that contributed to your success.

b) Weaknesses: Reflect on areas where you feel less confident or where you struggle. Consider skills or qualities that you would like to improve or those that have hindered your progress in the past. Look for patterns or recurring challenges that may indicate areas of weakness.

2. Feedback from Others:

Another valuable source for identifying your strengths and weaknesses is feedback from others. Seek input from trustworthy and objective sources such as mentors colleagues friends or family members.

a) Feedback on Strengths: Ask others about the skills qualities or abilities they admire or appreciate in you. Inquire about specific instances where they have noticed you excel in certain areas. Their observations can shed light on strengths you may not have recognized or fully acknowledged.

b) Feedback on Weaknesses: Request constructive feedback on areas where you could improve. Open yourself up to criticism and be receptive to suggestions for growth. Pay attention to recurring themes in the feedback you receive as they may indicate areas of weakness that need attention.

3. Assessment Tools:

Various assessment tools can provide insights into your strengths and weaknesses. These tools typically involve questionnaires assessments or quizzes designed to evaluate different aspects of your personality skills or aptitudes.

a) Personality Assessments: These assessments such as the Myers-Briggs Type Indicator (MBTI) or the Big Five Personality Traits can help you understand your core personality traits and how they influence your strengths and weaknesses.

b) Skill Assessments: Skill-based assessments like the StrengthsFinder or CliftonStrengths focus specifically on identifying and categorizing your top strengths. These assessments can give you a clear understanding of the areas where you naturally excel.

4. Professional Evaluation:

If you have access to professional evaluation tools or resources they can provide valuable insights into your strengths and weaknesses. These evaluations are often conducted by career counselors coaches or experts in the field.

a) Performance Reviews: Review past performance evaluations to gather information on your strengths and weaknesses as perceived by your supervisors or colleagues. Note any consistent feedback or areas of improvement mentioned.

b) Career Assessments: Career assessments such as vocational tests or career aptitude tests evaluate your interests skills and values to determine which career paths align with your strengths. These assessments can help you identify areas where you may have a natural inclination or a higher aptitude.

Conducting a Self-Assessment:

Conducting a self-assessment is an invaluable tool for personal growth and development. It involves taking the time to reflect on various aspects of your life skills and abilities. The purpose of a self-assessment is to gain a deeper understanding of yourself and assess your current strengths weaknesses and areas for improvement.

To conduct a self-assessment start by setting aside dedicated time in a quiet and comfortable space. Take a step back from your daily routine and begin to reflect on different areas of your life such as your personal relationships career hobbies and overall well-being.

Recognizing Areas for Improvement:

During the self-assessment process it is essential to recognize and acknowledge areas in which you can improve. This could be in your personal life such as communication skills time management or emotional intelligence. It could also be in your professional life like enhancing technical skills leadership abilities or adaptability to change.

Identifying these areas for improvement is not about self-criticism or dwelling on failures but rather about embracing growth opportunities and making positive changes. The self-assessment helps you become aware of areas where you can invest time energy and resources to enhance your overall effectiveness and satisfaction.

Leveraging Your Natural Talents:

While recognizing areas for improvement is crucial it is equally important to identify and leverage your natural talents and strengths. Understanding your unique abilities allows you to focus on areas where you naturally excel increasing your chances of success and fulfillment.

Leveraging your natural talents involves harnessing your inherent skills and traits to achieve your goals. It is about finding opportunities that align with your strengths and constantly seeking ways to further develop and utilize these qualities. By understanding and utilizing your natural talents you can optimize your performance enhance your confidence and approach challenges with a sense of empowerment.

In conclusion conducting a self-assessment involves reflecting on different aspects of your life recognizing areas for improvement and leveraging your natural talents. It is a powerful self-reflection tool that contributes to personal growth and allows you to make meaningful changes to lead a more fulfilling and successful life.

Chapter 3: Setting Clear Goals

In Chapter 3 we delve into the importance of setting clear goals and the impact they can have on our lives. By definition goals are targets or objectives that we aim to achieve. They provide direction purpose and motivation helping us stay focused and driven in various aspects of our lives such as personal development career relationships health and more.

Setting clear goals is essential because it allows us to outline specific outcomes we desire visualize our path to success and take actionable steps to reach those outcomes. Without clear goals we may find ourselves wandering aimlessly or being easily swayed by external factors which can hinder our progress and overall satisfaction.

Here are some key reasons why setting clear goals is important:

1. Clarity and Focus: Clear goals give us a sense of clarity and direction. When we have a clear target in mind it becomes easier to identify the necessary steps and actions needed to achieve that goal. This clarity helps us prioritize our time and efforts avoiding distractions and maintaining focus on what truly matters.

2. Motivation and Drive: Goals create motivation. When we set realistic and meaningful goals they serve as a powerful driving force that keeps us motivated and committed progress provides a sense of fulfillment and satisfaction boosting our confidence and giving us momentum to continue working towards our goals.

4. Overcoming Obstacles: Goals help us navigate obstacles. Challenges and setbacks are inevitable on any journey but when we have clear goals in place we are better equipped to overcome them. We can troubleshoot strategize and adapt our plans to adjust to unexpected circumstances ultimately finding alternative solutions to reach our desired outcomes.

5. Enhanced Decision Making: Clear goals aid decision-making processes. When we have well-defined goals it becomes easier to make choices that align with those goals. We can evaluate opportunities and weigh the potential impact they may have on our objectives. This focus allows us to make more informed decisions avoiding those that may derail our progress or lead us astray.

To set clear goals effectively consider the following tips:

1. Be Specific: Clearly define what you want to achieve. The more specific your goal the easier it will be to create a plan and take actionable steps towards it.

2. Set Measurable Objectives: Make your goals measurable by incorporating concrete criteria that can be tracked. This enables you to assess progress and determine if adjustments need to be

made.

3. Make Them Attainable: Be realistic and consider your resources capabilities and timeline. Setting unattainable goals can lead to frustration and disappointment while attainable goals provide a sense of achievement and encouragement.

4. Write Them Down: Putting your goals in writing increases commitment and provides a reference point. It helps solidify your intentions and serves as a constant reminder of what you are working towards.

5. Break Them Down: Divide larger goals into smaller manageable tasks or milestones. Breaking goals down into more manageable pieces helps prevent overwhelm and provides a clear roadmap to follow.

Remember setting clear goals is a continuous and evolving process. It's important to regularly review and reassess your goals as you progress making adjustments as needed. By doing so you can stay aligned with your aspirations and maximize your chances of success in all areas of your life.

Defining Short-term and Long-term Goals:

Short-term goals are specific achievable objectives that you aim to accomplish within a relatively brief period typically spanning a few days to a year. These goals help you stay focused motivated and provide a sense of accomplishment along the way. Examples of short-term goals could be completing a project improving a specific skill or reaching a certain milestone in your personal or professional life.

On the other hand long-term goals are broader objectives that you strive to achieve over. Break it down: Divide your long-term goals into smaller manageable milestones that you can work towards in the short term. This will make your goals more achievable and less overwhelming.

3. Identify necessary actions: Determine the actions and tasks required to reach each milestone. These actions can include acquiring new skills networking setting aside time for self-improvement or seeking additional education.

4. Set deadlines: Assign realistic deadlines to each milestone and action item. This helps create a sense of urgency and ensures that you stay on track.

5. Prioritize and set targets: Prioritize your milestones and actions based on their importance and impact. Set measurable targets for each enabling you to gauge your progress and make any necessary adjustments.

Setting Realistic and Achievable Targets:

When setting targets it's crucial to be realistic to maintain motivation and ensure success. Here are some tips for setting realistic and achievable targets:

1. Assess your capabilities: Evaluate your current abilities available resources and the time you can commit to your goals.

Consider any constraints or limitations that may affect your progress.

2. Break your goals into small steps: Break your goals down into smaller more manageable tasks. This makes them easier to accomplish and provides a sense of progress.

3. Consider timeframes: Set reasonable timeframes for completing each step or milestone. Be mindful of external factors that may affect your progress such as work or personal commitments.

4. Be flexible: Adapt your targets as you progress. Sometimes unforeseen circumstances or unexpected challenges may arise. Adjust your targets to remain realistic while keeping your ultimate goal in sight.

5. Celebrate milestones: Celebrate your achievements along the way. Recognizing and rewarding your progress boosts motivation and encourages further success.

In summary by defining short-term and long-term goals creating a roadmap to success and setting realistic and achievable targets you can effectively work towards accomplishing the goals you have set for yourself. This systematic approach enhances focus keeps you motivated and enables you to track your progress ultimately leading to greater success.

Chapter 4: Creating a Learning Plan

Creating a learning plan is essential to achieving your educational goals. It helps you stay organized stay on track and ensures that you make efficient progress towards learning new skills or acquiring knowledge. In this chapter we will explore the detailed steps involved in creating an effective learning plan.

Step 1: Define Your Learning Goals

The first step in creating a learning plan is to clearly define your learning goals. Ask yourself what you want to achieve through your learning efforts. This could be acquiring new skills gaining knowledge in a specific subject area or improving existing skills. Make your goals specific measurable achievable relevant and time-bound (SMART goals).

Step 2: Assess Your Current Level

Once you have defined your learning goals it is important to assess your current level of knowledge or skills in the chosen area. This self-assessment will provide you with a baseline to start from and help you identify any gaps that need to be addressed. You can use various methods such as self-reflection quizzes tests or seeking feedback from others to evaluate your current level.

Step 3: Determine Learning Resources

Identify the learning resources that will help you achieve your goals. This could include textbooks online courses video tutorials podcasts articles or mentorship programs. Take into account your preferred learning style and choose resources that align with it. Also consider the credibility and quality of the resources to ensure that you are learning accurate and up-to-date information.

Step 4: Set a Schedule

Creating a schedule is crucial to stay disciplined and allocate dedicated time for your learning activities. Determine how much time you can commit to learning each day or week and create a realistic schedule. Divide your learning plan into smaller milestones or chunks and set deadlines for each milestone. This will help you track your progress and stay motivated.

Step 5: Break Down Learning into Manageable Steps

Break down your learning goals into manageable steps. Start with the foundational concepts or skills and gradually progress to more advanced topics. This step-by-step approach will help you build a solid understanding of the subject matter and prevent overwhelm. Create a checklist or timeline to keep track of each step completed.

Step 6: Seek Support and Accountability

Find a learning buddy study group or mentor who can provide support guidance and accountability. Discuss your learning goals with them and mutually agree on ways to hold each other accountable. Regular check-ins discussions and sharing progress can significantly enhance your learning experience and motivation.

Step 7: Measure Progress and Make Adjustments

Regularly monitor your progress and assess how well you are meeting your learning goals. Use different metrics such as completed milestones quizzes or self-assessments to measure your progress. Reflect on your learning experience and make necessary adjustments to your plan if required. This could involve reallocating more time to challenging topics or seeking additional resources.

Step 8: Celebrate Achievements

Celebrate your achievements along the way. Acknowledging your progress and accomplishments will keep you motivated and energized to continue pursuing your learning goals. Take time to appreciate the effort and dedication you put into your learning journey.

By following these steps you can create a well-structured learning plan that aligns with your goals and maximizes your chances of success. Remember that flexibility is key and it's important to adapt your plan as needed. Stay committed embrace the process and enjoy the satisfaction of continuous learning and growth.

Researching Learning Resources and Opportunities:

Researching learning resources and opportunities involves finding reliable and relevant sources of information to enhance your knowledge and skills. It's important to seek out resources that align with your learning goals and are reputable and well-regarded in the field you're studying.

To start you can utilize online search engines libraries educational platforms and professional networks to find resources such as books articles research papers online courses tutorials podcasts webinars and workshops. Pay attention to the credibility and authority of the sources and consider reviews and recommendations from trusted individuals or organizations.

Structuring Your Learning Schedule:

Structuring your learning schedule is crucial for effective and consistent learning. Without a well-organized plan it's easy to get overwhelmed or sidetracked. Here are some steps to structure your learning schedule:

1. Set Clear Learning Goals: Define what you want to achieve and break it down into smaller manageable tasks that can be completed within realistic timeframes.

2. Prioritize Your Tasks: Identify the most important and urgent tasks and allocate sufficient time for them. Consider using techniques such as the Eisenhower Matrix to prioritize your activities.

3. Create a Schedule: Set aside specific blocks of time in your calendar dedicated to learning activities. Determine the duration and frequency based on your availability and learning needs. Consistency is key so aim for regular study sessions.

4. Allocate Time for Review and Reflection: Include time for reviewing previously learned materials and reflecting on your progress. This helps reinforce learning and identify areas that require further attention.

5. Be Flexible: Allow some flexibility in your schedule to accommodate unexpected events or changes. Adapt your plan if needed but try to maintain overall consistency.

Balancing Theory and Practice:

Balancing theory and practice is important for a well-rounded learning experience. Theory provides a conceptual understanding of a subject while practice allows you to apply that knowledge in real-world scenarios. Here are some ways to achieve a balance:

1. Start with Foundations: Begin by gaining a strong theoretical understanding of the subject matter. This can be accomplished through reading books attending lectures or taking online courses.

2. Practical Application: Once you have grasped the theory practice applying it in practical situations. This can involve projects case studies simulations or real-world experiences. Seek opportunities like internships volunteering or collaborating with others in your field.

3. Reflect and Analyze: Regularly reflect on your practical experiences and analyze how they align with the theories you've learned. Consider what worked well what challenges you faced and how you can improve.

4. Iterate and Iterate: Use feedback and insights gained from practical experience to refine and adjust your understanding of the theory. Consider revisiting relevant concepts to deepen your understanding.

5. Seek Feedback and Mentors: Engage with mentors or experienced professionals who can provide guidance and feedback on your progress. Their insights can help you bridge the gap between theory and practice.

Remember finding the right balance between theory and practice is an iterative process that evolves as you continue to learn and gain experience.

Chapter 5: Effective Learning Techniques

In this chapter we will explore various effective learning techniques that can help improve your learning process and enhance your overall understanding and retention of information. These techniques have been widely researched and proven to be beneficial for learners of all ages and across various subjects. By incorporating these techniques into your study routine you can maximize your learning potential and achieve better academic outcomes.

1. Spaced Repetition: Spaced repetition is a learning technique that involves reviewing information at increasing intervals over time. Instead of cramming all your studying into one session spacing out your repetitions allows for better long-term retention. By reviewing the material at strategic intervals you reinforce the memory and prevent forgetting. Tools like flashcards and spaced repetition software can be highly effective in implementing this technique.

2. Active Recall: Active recall is the process of retrieving information from memory rather than passively reviewing it. It involves actively engaging with the material by attempting

to recall key points concepts or answers to questions. This technique has been shown to significantly improve long-term retention compared to passive reading or re-reading. You can practice active recall by using flashcards quizzing yourself or explaining concepts aloud.

3. Elaboration: Elaboration involves expanding on the information being learned by connecting it to existing knowledge or creating meaningful associations. By explaining concepts in your own words or relating them to real-life examples you deepen your understanding and create more robust mental connections. This technique aids in information retention and comprehension.

4. Interleaving: Interleaving is the practice of mixing different topics or problem types during study sessions. Rather than focusing on a single topic for an extended period interleaving requires you to switch between different subjects or types of problems. This technique promotes active learning and increases the capacity for transfer of knowledge. By challenging yourself to apply different concepts in diverse contexts you develop a more flexible and integrated understanding.

5. Dual Coding: Dual coding involves combining visual and verbal encoding of information. By representing concepts both visually and through accompanying text or verbal explanations you engage multiple cognitive processes simultaneously. This dual representation enhances comprehension and retention as well as facilitates information recall. Techniques such as creating diagrams concept maps or visual mnemonics can be employed for effective dual coding.

6. Retrieval Practice: Retrieval practice focuses on actively retrieving information from memory to strengthen the memory traces associated with the learned material. This technique involves deliberate self-testing practicing retrieving information without aid and reviewing the gaps in your knowledge. By repeatedly retrieving the information you reinforce the memory pathways and improve long-term retention.

7. Metacognition: Metacognition refers to the awareness and understanding of one's own learning process. It involves self-reflection monitoring of learning progress and evaluation of learning strategies. By regularly assessing your learning methods and adapting them based on how well they are working for you you can optimize your learning process and identify areas for improvement.

It is important to note that these techniques work best when combined and tailored to your preferences and learning style. Experiment with different strategies adapt them to your needs and find what works best for you. By implementing these effective learning techniques you can enhance your learning experience and achieve greater academic success.

Active Learning Strategies:

Active learning is an approach that involves engaging students in the learning process by encouraging them to think question discuss and apply what they have learned. Here are some effective active learning strategies:

1. Group discussions: Encourage students to discuss concepts and ideas with their peers. This promotes critical thinking problem-solving and active participation.

2. Problem-solving activities: Engage students in hands-on activities that require them to solve problems or complete tasks. This helps them apply their knowledge in practical scenarios.

3. Case studies: Present real-life or hypothetical scenarios for students to analyze and apply their knowledge. This enhances critical thinking and decision-making skills.

4. Role-playing: Assign roles to students related to a particular subject or topic. This allows them to immerse themselves in different perspectives and promote a deeper understanding of the material.

5. Peer teaching: Encourage students to explain concepts or teach their peers. This not only reinforces their understanding but also fosters collaboration and communication skills.

Memory Improvement Techniques:
   Improving memory can greatly benefit learning and retention. Here are some techniques to enhance memory:

1. Visualization: Create mental images or visualizations to associate with new information. This helps in encoding and recalling the material.

2. Chunking: Break down complex information into smaller manageable chunks. This makes it easier to remember and

retrieve the information.

3. Mnemonic devices: Use mnemonic strategies like acronyms acrostics or rhymes to remember information. For example "ROY G. BIV" to remember the colors of the rainbow (Red Orange Yellow Green Blue Indigo Violet).

4. Spaced repetition: Review information at regular intervals over time. This helps reinforce memory and prevents forgetting.

5. Association: Connect new information to previously learned knowledge or create associations with familiar concepts. This provides context and facilitates retrieval.

Effective Note-taking Methods:
   Taking effective notes during lectures or while studying can help with retention and comprehension. Here are some note-taking methods:

1. Cornell method: Divide your page into three sections - a narrow left column for cues or key points a wider right column for detailed notes and a bottom section for summaries or questions.

2. Mind mapping: Use visual techniques to connect main ideas and subtopics. This method helps you see the relationships between ideas and organize information hierarchically.

3. Outline method: Structure your notes using headings sub-headings and bullet points. This method helps you capture the main ideas and their supporting details.

4. Flowchart method: Use flowcharts or diagrams to illustrate processes or relationships between ideas. This visual representation aids understanding and recall.

5. Abbreviations and symbols: Develop a set of abbreviations and symbols to save time while taking notes. This allows for faster capture of information during lectures.

Remember the effectiveness of these strategies and techniques may vary depending on individual learning styles so it's essential to experiment and find what works best for you.

Chapter 6: Seeking Feedback and Guidance

In any endeavor seeking feedback and guidance is crucial for growth and improvement. It allows individuals to gain fresh perspectives identify blind spots and learn from others' experiences. This chapter delves deep into the importance of seeking feedback and guidance providing insights on how to approach it effectively.

Section 1: Why Seeking Feedback and Guidance Matters

1.1 The Power of Feedback: Feedback is a valuable tool for personal and professional growth. It provides insights into one's strengths and weaknesses highlighting areas for improvement. Constructive feedback helps individuals refine their skills enhance performance and build self-awareness.

1.2 Learning from Others: Guidance from experienced individuals can be immensely beneficial. It allows individuals to acquire knowledge gain insights and tap into lessons learned by those who have walked a similar path. Learning from others' successes and failures can help avoid common pitfalls and accelerate growth.

Section 2: Approaching Feedback and Guidance

2.1 Establishing Trust: Building trust is essential for effective feedback and guidance. Create an environment where people feel safe and comfortable providing honest and constructive feedback. Foster an open and non-judgmental atmosphere that encourages dialogue and learning.

2.2 Being Specific: When seeking feedback be clear and specific about what you want to learn or improve upon. Ask targeted questions that address your concerns or areas of interest. This allows the feedback provider to provide more focused insights and guidance.

2.3 Active Listening: Actively listen and be receptive to feedback. Maintain an open mind and avoid becoming defensive or dismissive. Asking follow-up questions to seek clarification and demonstrating genuine interest shows your commitment to learning and growth.

2.4 Diverse Perspectives: Seek feedback from a diverse range of individuals. Different perspectives offer unique insights and alternative approaches. Engage with people from different backgrounds experiences and expertise to gain a well-rounded understanding.

Section 3: Applying Feedback and Guidance

3.1 Reflect and Evaluate: After receiving feedback take the time to reflect upon it. Analyze the insights provided evaluate their validity and identify actionable steps for improvement. Be objective in assessing your strengths and weaknesses and use the feedback as a catalyst for growth.

3.2 Implementing Changes: Once you have identified areas for improvement take action. Develop a plan and implement changes based on the feedback and guidance received. This could involve acquiring new skills adjusting behaviors or seeking additional support to enhance your development.

3.3 Continuous Improvement: Seek feedback regularly and embrace a continuous improvement mindset. Learning is an ongoing process and seeking guidance should be a consistent practice. Regularly evaluate progress adapt to evolving circumstances and refine your goals based on the feedback received.

Section 4: Giving Feedback and Guidance

4.1 Reciprocity: Just as it is crucial to seek feedback and guidance providing it to others fosters a collaborative and supportive environment. Offer feedback to peers colleagues or mentees by following the principles discussed earlier. Create a feedback culture that encourages growth and development for all.

4.2 Constructive Criticism: When giving feedback focus on constructive criticism. Frame feedback in a way that is supportive specific and actionable. Provide examples and suggestions for improvement while maintaining a positive and encouraging tone.

4.3 Impactful Guidance: When offering guidance draw upon your own experiences and knowledge. Share insights lessons learned and practical advice that can help others navigate challenges or develop their skills. Offer guidance within your area of expertise and communicate with empathy and understanding.

By actively seeking feedback and guidance individuals can unlock their full potential accelerate their development and achieve meaningful growth. It is a process that requires openness humility and a genuine commitment to continuous learning. Embrace feedback as a gift and leverage the guidance of others to amplify your progress on your journey toward success.

Chapter 7: Developing Discipline and Consistency

Introduction:

In any endeavor whether it is personal or professional discipline and consistency are key factors that contribute to success. Developing discipline and consistency requires a focused effort and a willingness to adhere to certain practices and routines. This chapter explores why discipline and consistency are vital as well as strategies and techniques to help you cultivate these qualities.

1. Understanding the Importance of Discipline and Consistency:

Discipline refers to the ability to stay committed and focused on a task or goal even when faced with challenges or distractions. Consistency on the other hand involves maintaining a steady and reliable approach towards your actions and behavior. These two qualities are highly interlinked as discipline enables you to consistently follow through with your plans and obligations.

Discipline and consistency are crucial for several reasons:

a. Achievement of Goals: Discipline helps you set clear goals and work towards them consistently. Without discipline it is easy to get distracted or give up on your objectives.

b. Personal Growth: Developing discipline and consistency fosters personal growth and self-improvement. It allows you to push past your comfort zone and develop new skills and habits.

c. Professional Success: In the workplace discipline and consistency contribute to higher productivity efficient time management and reliability which can lead to career advancement.

d. Building Relationships: Consistency in behavior and actions helps build trust and reliability in relationships both personal and professional.

2. Cultivating Discipline and Consistency:

a. Set Clear Goals: Establishing clear and specific goals provides direction and motivation. Write down your goals and break them into smaller achievable tasks creating a roadmap for success.

b. Develop a Routine: Consistency thrives in structured routines. Create a daily or weekly schedule that includes dedicated time for important tasks self-care and relaxation.

c. Prioritize and Eliminate Distractions: Identify distractions that hinder your progress and develop strategies to manage them. This may involve setting boundaries creating a focused work environment or utilizing time management techniques.

d. Practice Self-Control: Discipline often requires resisting short-term temptations for long-term benefits. Develop strategies to strengthen your self-control such as mindfulness meditation or accountability systems.

e. Focus on Habits: Building consistent habits leads to discipline. Start by identifying positive habits that align with your goals and slowly incorporate them into your routine. Track your progress and celebrate small victories along the way.

f. Build a Support System: Surround yourself with individuals who share your values and goals. They can provide accountability motivation and support when maintaining discipline becomes challenging.

g. Learn from Setbacks: Discipline and consistency are not always easy and setbacks are inevitable. Rather than viewing setbacks as failures learn from them and adapt your approach. Use them as opportunities to grow and improve.

3. Overcoming Challenges:

Developing discipline and consistency can be challenging due to various factors such as lack of motivation external distractions or self-doubt. Here are some strategies to overcome these challenges:

a. Find Your Why: Understand the deeper reasons behind your goals and connect with them emotionally. This will provide long-lasting motivation.

b. Break Tasks into Smaller Steps: Large tasks can be overwhelming and lead to procrastination. Break them down into smaller manageable steps to maintain momentum and reduce stress.

c. Create Accountability: Share your goals with others or seek an accountability partner. Knowing that someone will hold you responsible can help you stay focused and consistent.

d. Practice Self-Care: Taking care of your physical and mental well-being is crucial for maintaining discipline and consistency. Ensure you get enough rest exercise regularly eat a balanced diet and manage stress effectively.

e. Practice Mindfulness: Cultivate mindfulness to help you stay present and focused on the task at hand. This can enhance your ability to prioritize and resist distractions.

f. Celebrate Progress: Acknowledge and celebrate even the smallest achievements along your journey. Recognizing progress boosts motivation and reinforces the positive habits you are developing.

Conclusion:

Discipline and consistency are essential qualities that contribute to personal and professional growth. By understanding their importance and implementing strategies to develop these qualities you can enhance your chances of success in all aspects of life. Remember developing discipline and consistency is a lifelong journey that requires dedication practice and self-reflection.

1. The Power of Habits:

Habits are powerful routines that we engage in without conscious thought. They shape our behavior and play a significant role in our daily lives. Habits have a profound impact on our personal and professional success as they can be either positive or negative.

Positive habits can help us achieve our goals improve our productivity and enhance our overall well-being. For example practicing regular exercise maintaining a healthy diet or dedicating time for self-reflection can lead to long-term positive outcomes. On the other hand negative habits such as procrastination excessive screen time or unhealthy eating patterns can hinder our progress and limit our potential.

Understanding the power of habits allows us to take control

of our lives. By consciously designing and nurturing positive habits we can create a more fulfilling and successful future for ourselves.

2. Building a Consistent Practice Routine:

A consistent practice routine is essential for honing skills achieving mastery and making progress in any area of life. Whether it's learning a musical instrument developing a fitness regimen or enhancing a professional skill consistency is key.

To build a consistent practice routine consider the following steps:

a. Set clear goals: Define specific and realistic goals that you want to achieve through your practice. Having a clear vision of what you want to accomplish helps you stay motivated and focused.

b. Create a schedule: Establish a regular schedule for your practice sessions. Consistency is vital so allocate dedicated time each day or week to work on your chosen skill.

c. Break it down: Divide your practice into manageable chunks. Breaking down large tasks or skills into smaller achievable steps makes the practice routine more manageable. This way progress becomes evident boosting motivation and confidence.

d. Hold yourself accountable: Find ways to hold yourself accountable for sticking to your practice routine. This could involve tracking your progress sharing your goals with a friend or mentor or using habit-tracking apps.

e. Maintain variety and adaptability: While consistency is crucial it's also important to keep your practice routine interesting and adaptable. Incorporate different techniques exercises or challenges to keep yourself engaged and prevent boredom or plateauing.

3. Overcoming Procrastination and Distractions:
   Procrastination and distractions are common obstacles that prevent us from accomplishing our goals and maintaining a consistent practice routine. However there are strategies you can employ to overcome these challenges:

a. Identify the root cause: Understand why you tend to procrastinate or get easily distracted. It could be due to fear of failure lack of interest overwhelm or a habituated response. Recognizing the underlying reasons helps address them effectively.

b. Create a conducive environment: Minimize distractions by creating an environment that supports your practice. This may involve finding a quiet space putting your phone on silent or using website blockers to avoid online distractions.

c. Set specific time limits: Break your practice sessions into smaller focused blocks of time. By setting a specific time limit (e.g 25 minutes known as the Pomodoro Technique you can work with greater focus and prioritize your tasks effectively.

d. Develop self-discipline: Train yourself to resist immediate gratification and prioritize long-term benefits. Practice delaying distractions by using techniques like "just five more minutes" or creating rewards for completing tasks.

e. Cultivate mindfulness: Practice being present and aware of your thoughts and actions. Mindfulness helps you recognize when you get pulled into distractions allowing you to refocus and redirect your attention back to your practice.

By understanding the power of habits building a consistent practice routine and learning how to overcome procrastination and distractions you can maximize your potential accomplish your goals and lead a more balanced and fulfilling life.

Chapter 8: Embracing Failure and Learning from Mistakes

Introduction:

Failure is often seen as a negative outcome something to be avoided at all costs. However in reality failure can be a valuable learning experience and a stepping stone to success. In this chapter we will explore the importance of embracing failure and how to learn from mistakes.

1. Changing Mindsets:

The first step in embracing failure is to shift our mindset and view failure as a necessary part of the learning process. Instead of fearing failure we should see it as an opportunity for growth and improvement. This shift in mindset allows us to approach challenges with more resilience and openness.

2. Creating a Safe Environment:

To encourage a culture of learning from mistakes it is important to create a safe environment where individuals feel comfortable taking risks and making errors. This can be achieved through open communication non-judgmental feedback and emphasizing the value of learning over perfection.

3. Analyzing Failures:

When faced with failure it is crucial to take the time to reflect and analyze what went wrong. This involves identifying the root causes examining the decision-making process and considering alternative approaches. By understanding the reasons behind the failure we can make informed adjustments and avoid repeating the same mistakes in the future.

4. Extracting Lessons:

Every failure provides valuable lessons that can contribute to personal and professional growth. It is important to extract these lessons by identifying the specific skills knowledge or strategies that need improvement. By reflecting on our failures we can gain valuable insights that can be applied to future endeavors.

5. Developing Resilience:

Embracing failure requires developing resilience the ability to bounce back from setbacks and keep moving forward. Resilience is cultivated through a combination of self-belief perseverance and a positive mindset. By building resilience we can navigate failures with greater resilience and determination.

6. Iterative Approach:

Learning from mistakes involves adopting an iterative approach where we continuously refine and improve our strategies based on feedback and experience. This iterative process allows us to make incremental progress and adapt our approach as we encounter failures and setbacks. It emphasizes the importance of constant learning and adaptation.

7. Celebrating Small Wins:

While failure is an integral part of growth it is also important to celebrate small wins along the way. Recognizing and acknowledging progress no matter how small boosts morale and motivates continued effort. Celebrating small wins also helps maintain a positive mindset and reinforces the belief that success is attainable despite setbacks.

8. Cultivating a Growth Mindset:

Lastly embracing failure requires cultivating a growth mindset a belief that abilities and intelligence can be developed through effort and perseverance. A growth mindset recognizes that failure is not indicative of fixed limitations but rather an opportunity for improvement. By adopting a growth mindset we can overcome fear of failure and unlock our full potential.

Changing Your Perception of Failure:

Changing your perception of failure is crucial in overcoming setbacks and achieving personal growth. Instead of viewing failure as something negative or to be avoided at all costs it's important to reframe it as a valuable learning experience. Failure is not an endpoint but rather a stepping stone towards success.

Analyzing Mistakes and Extracting Lessons:

When faced with setbacks or mistakes it's essential to take the time to analyze them and extract valuable lessons. Instead of dwelling on the negativity or beating yourself up over the errors approach them with a curious and open mindset. Ask yourself questions like: What went wrong? What could I have done differently? What can I learn from this experience?

By actively reflecting on your mistakes you can gain insights into your actions decisions and thought processes. This self-reflection leads to self-awareness and can help you identify patterns or behaviors that may have contributed to the setback. It allows you to pinpoint areas of improvement and make changes for future endeavors.

Turning Setbacks into Opportunities for Growth:
Setbacks can be seen as opportunities for growth and development. Instead of allowing setbacks to define you or hinder your progress consider them as chances to learn adapt and become stronger. Embracing setbacks with a growth mindset can empower you to find innovative solutions develop resilience and cultivate a positive attitude towards challenges.

Think about setbacks as detours rather than roadblocks. It's essential to assess the situation identify alternative strategies and adjust your approach accordingly. By doing so you can turn setbacks into stepping stones towards success. Each setback provides an opportunity to learn grow and build upon your experiences ultimately leading to personal and professional development.

To summarize changing your perception of failure analyzing mistakes and turning setbacks into growth opportunities are essential elements in navigating setbacks and fostering personal growth. By embracing failure extracting lessons and adapting to setbacks you can cultivate resilience develop new skills and achieve your goals. Remember setbacks are not a sign of failure but an opportunity for growth and progress.

Chapter 9: Enhancing Problem-Solving and Critical Thinking Skills

In today's complex and fast-paced world being able to think critically and solve problems effectively is a highly valuable skill set. Whether in personal or professional settings the ability to analyze situations make informed decisions and devise effective solutions is crucial for success. In this chapter we will explore various techniques and strategies that can enhance problem-solving and critical thinking skills.

Section 1: Developing Analytical and Logical Thinking

Analytical and logical thinking are essential components of problem-solving and critical thinking. These skills involve the ability to break down complex problems into smaller more manageable parts identify patterns and relationships and apply logical reasoning to arrive at sound conclusions. Here are some techniques to develop these skills:

1.1. Recognizing Patterns: One effective way to enhance analytical thinking is by recognizing patterns in data or information. Patterns often provide insights and can help identify underlying causes or connections that may not be immediately apparent.

By actively seeking patterns and making connections you can develop a more holistic understanding of the problem and generate creative solutions.

1.2. Analyzing Cause and Effect: Developing the ability to analyze cause and effect relationships is crucial for effective problem-solving. By understanding the interdependencies between different variables and factors you can identify the root causes of the problem and devise solutions that address these underlying issues. This involves asking questions such as "Why did this happen?" and "What are the consequences of this action?"

1.3. Applying Logical Reasoning: Logical reasoning involves using deductive and inductive reasoning to draw conclusions based on evidence and facts. Deductive reasoning starts with general principles or theories and applies them to specific situations while inductive reasoning involves drawing general conclusions based on specific observations. By practicing logical reasoning you can improve your ability to evaluate arguments identify fallacies and make well-reasoned decisions.

Section 2: Effective Decision-making Strategies

Effective decision-making is a critical aspect of problem-solving. It involves the ability to assess alternatives evaluate risks and benefits and make informed choices based on available information. Here are some strategies to enhance decision-making skills:

2.1. Gathering and Analyzing Information: Effective decision-making relies on gathering and analyzing relevant information. This may involve conducting research collecting data consulting experts and considering multiple perspectives. By ensuring that you have a comprehensive and accurate understanding of the problem you can make better-informed decisions.

2.2. Evaluating Risks and Rewards: Every decision involves some level of risk and it is important to evaluate both the potential benefits and the potential consequences before making a choice. Consider the short-term and long-term implications of your decision assess the likelihood of success or failure and weigh the potential risks against the potential rewards.

2.3. Using Decision-Making Models: Decision-making models provide structured approaches to guide the decision-making process. One commonly used model is the rational decision-making model which involves identifying goals generating alternatives evaluating alternatives based on criteria and selecting the best option. Other models such as the intuitive decision-making model or the satisficing model can also be useful in specific situations.

2.4. Considering Ethical and Moral Implications: Ethical considerations should play a significant role in decision-making. Assess the ethical implications of different alternatives and evaluate whether the choices align with your values and principles. Consider the potential impact on stakeholders and the broader society when making decisions.

Section 3: Problem-Solving Techniques

Problem-solving is the process of finding effective solutions to complex issues or challenges. It involves identifying the problem generating potential solutions evaluating and selecting the best course of action and implementing the solution. Here are some techniques to enhance problem-solving skills:

3.1. Defining the Problem: The first step in problem-solving is clearly defining the problem. Take the time to understand the root causes underlying issues and desired outcomes. This involves asking questions seeking different viewpoints and gathering relevant information.

3.2. Generating Alternative Solutions: Once the problem is defined it is important to generate a range of potential solutions. Encourage creativity and divergent thinking by brainstorming ideas considering different perspectives and challenging assumptions. Quantity is important at this stage – aim to generate as many potential solutions as possible.

3.3. Evaluating and Selecting Solutions: After generating alternative solutions it is necessary to evaluate and select the best course of action. Consider the advantages and disadvantages of each solution assess their feasibility and weigh them against predetermined criteria or goals. Engage in critical thinking to ensure that the chosen solution aligns with the problem definition and desired outcomes.

3.4. Implementing and Evaluating the Solution: Once a solution is selected it needs to be implemented effectively. Develop a clear action plan assign responsibilities and ensure effective communication. Monitoring and evaluating the solution's effectiveness is crucial to make any necessary adjustments and learn from the experience.

Conclusion:

Enhancing problem-solving and critical thinking skills is essential for success in various aspects of life. By developing analytical and logical thinking using effective decision-making strategies and employing problem-solving techniques individuals can enhance their ability to tackle complex problems and make informed choices. Continuous practice self-reflection and an open mindset are key to improving these skills. With these enhanced skills individuals are better equipped to face challenges find creative solutions and make sound decisions in both personal and professional contexts.

Chapter 10: Fostering Creativity and Innovation

Fostering Creativity and Innovation exploring the topics of cultivating a creative mindset techniques for generating innovative ideas and overcoming creative blocks.

1. Cultivating a Creative Mindset:
   In order to foster creativity and innovation it is crucial to develop a creative mindset. Here are some key considerations:

a. Embrace Curiosity: Curiosity is the fuel for creativity. Maintain a sense of wonder and actively seek out new knowledge and experiences. Ask probing questions and explore different perspectives to broaden your thinking.

b. Embrace Failure: Understand that failure is part of the creative process. Embrace it as a valuable learning opportunity that can lead to breakthroughs. Adopt a growth mindset where failures are seen as stepping stones to success.

c. Embrace Ambiguity: Creative thinking thrives when you can embrace uncertainty. Be comfortable with exploring multiple paths and solutions even if they are unconventional. Embrace ambiguity and use it as a catalyst for innovation.

d. Foster an Open Mind: Be open to new ideas diverse perspectives and alternative solutions. Avoid judgment and create an environment that encourages collaboration and the sharing of ideas.

2. Techniques for Generating Innovative Ideas:
   Generating innovative ideas is an essential part of the creative process. Here are some techniques to help stimulate your creativity:

a. Brainstorming: Brainstorming is a popular technique involving the generation of ideas in a non-judgmental and open environment. Encourage free-thinking and explore a wide range of ideas no matter how wild or unconventional they may seem.

b. Mind Mapping: Mind mapping is a visual tool used to generate and organize ideas. Start with a central concept and then branch out adding related ideas and concepts. This technique helps to identify connections and uncover new perspectives.

c. SCAMPER Technique: SCAMPER is an acronym for Substitute Combine Adapt Modify Put to another use Eliminate Rearrange. It is a systematic way of exploring existing ideas and concepts and generating new ones by applying these different techniques.

d. Random Word Association: This technique involves connecting unrelated words or concepts to generate new ideas. Pick a random word and explore how it can be linked to a particular challenge or problem generating fresh perspectives and insights.

3. Overcoming Creative Blocks:

Creative blocks can hinder the creative process. Here are some strategies for addressing and overcoming them:

a. Take Breaks: Step away from the problem for a while and engage in a different activity. This can help you gain a fresh perspective and re-energize your creative thinking.

b. Seek Inspiration: Surround yourself with sources of inspiration. Read books articles or watch movies that stimulate your creativity. Engage in activities that inspire and excite you such as visiting museums or attending events.

c. Collaborate: Engage in collaborative work with others leveraging their unique perspectives and insights. Brainstorming with a group can help overcome individual creative blocks and inspire new ideas through collective thinking.

d. Practice Mindfulness: Cultivating mindfulness can help quiet your mind reduce stress and enhance your ability to be present and fully engage in the creative process.

e. Experiment and Explore: Don't be afraid to take risks and try new approaches. Embrace experimentation as often breakthrough ideas come from unconventional paths.

By understanding and implementing these strategies you can foster a creative mindset generate innovative ideas and overcome creative blocks. Remember that creativity like any skill can be nurtured and developed with intention and practice.

Chapter 11: Maintaining Focus and Managing Stress

In today's fast-paced world maintaining focus and managing stress are crucial skills for personal and professional success. This chapter will delve deeper into strategies for concentration and focus stress management techniques and achieving work-life balance.

1. Strategies for Concentration and Focus:

   To maintain focus and concentrate effectively consider implementing the following strategies:

a) Minimize distractions: Identify and remove any potential distractions in your environment. This could include turning off notifications on your electronic devices finding a quiet workspace or using noise-canceling headphones.

b) Practice mindfulness: Engage in mindfulness techniques such as meditation or deep breathing exercises to train your mind to stay present and focused on the task at hand.

c) Set clear goals: Clearly define your objectives and break them down into smaller manageable tasks. This will help you stay focused by providing a sense of direction and accomplishment.

d) Use time management techniques: Prioritize your tasks create to-do lists and allocate specific time blocks for different activities. Techniques like the Pomodoro Technique where you work in short sprints with frequent breaks can also help improve focus and productivity.

e) Utilize visualization: Visualize yourself successfully completing the task or project you're working on. This can enhance concentration and motivation.

2. Stress Management Techniques:
   To effectively manage stress consider incorporating the following techniques into your routine:

a) Exercise regularly: Engaging in physical activity releases endorphins which help reduce stress and improve mood. Aim for at least 30 minutes of moderate exercise most days of the week.

b) Practice relaxation techniques: Explore techniques like deep breathing exercises progressive muscle relaxation or guided imagery to elicit a relaxation response and reduce stress.

c) Maintain a healthy lifestyle: Ensure you're getting enough sleep eating a balanced diet and staying hydrated. These factors play a significant role in managing stress.

d) Seek support: Talk to friends family or a trusted professional about your stresses and concerns. Sharing your feelings can provide emotional relief and perspective.

e) Time management: Properly allocate your time by prioritizing tasks setting realistic deadlines and avoiding over-commitment. This reduces the stress of feeling overwhelmed or rushed.

3. Achieving Work-Life Balance:

Striking a balance between work and personal life is essential for overall well-being. Here are some tips to achieve work-life balance:

a) Set boundaries: Clearly define your work hours and establish limits on working outside of those designated times. Communicate these boundaries to your colleagues and avoid the temptation to constantly check work-related emails or messages.

b) Prioritize self-care: Make time for activities that promote self-care and relaxation such as hobbies exercise spending time with loved ones or pursuing personal interests. Self-care is crucial for preventing burnout and maintaining mental and emotional well-being.

c) Delegate and ask for help: Don't hesitate to delegate tasks or ask for assistance when feeling overwhelmed. Recognize that it's impossible to do everything on your own and seeking support can lighten the load.

d) Plan and schedule: Establish a routine and create a schedule that allows for a healthy balance between work and personal life.

Set aside dedicated blocks of time for family leisure activities or personal commitments.

e) Disconnect from technology: Take regular breaks from electronic devices to disconnect and focus on leisure activities or spending quality time with loved ones. Unplugging allows you to recharge and truly be present in the moment.

Remember that maintaining focus and managing stress are ongoing processes. Adapt these strategies to suit your unique circumstances and regularly evaluate their effectiveness. With practice you can cultivate greater focus reduce stress levels and achieve a more fulfilling work-life balance.

Chapter 12: Celebrating Progress and Continued Growth

In this chapter we will explore the importance of celebrating milestones and achievements reflecting on progress and cultivating lifelong learning habits. These practices are vital for personal and professional growth and they contribute to a fulfilling and successful life.

Section 1: Recognizing Milestones and Achievements

Milestones and achievements are significant events or accomplishments that mark progress and success. They can be small or big personal or professional and they play a crucial role in our motivation and self-esteem. Recognizing and celebrating these milestones is essential for several reasons:

1. Motivation: Celebrating achievements provides a boost of motivation to keep pursuing our goals. It reinforces the belief that hard work and dedication pay off.

2. Self-esteem: Acknowledging our accomplishments boosts our self-esteem and confidence. It validates our efforts and reminds us that we are capable of achieving great things.

3. Reflection: Celebrating milestones allows us to reflect on the journey we have undertaken. We can evaluate the strategies and actions that led to success and learn from any challenges faced along the way.

4. Inspiring others: By celebrating our achievements we become a source of inspiration for others. Our successes can motivate and encourage others to pursue their own goals and dreams.

Section 2: Reflecting on Progress

Reflection is a valuable practice that enables us to understand our growth and development. Taking the time to reflect on our progress allows us to:

1. Assess achievements: We can evaluate the goals we have achieved and the milestones we have reached. This assessment helps us understand the areas where we have excelled and those that require further attention.

2. Identify areas for improvement: Reflection helps us identify areas where we can improve and grow. By assessing our strengths and weaknesses we can create action plans to enhance our skills and knowledge.

3. Learn from mistakes: Reflecting on progress allows us to learn from any mistakes or setbacks we encountered. We can analyze what went wrong and identify strategies to prevent similar setbacks in the future.

4. Clarify intentions: Reflection offers an opportunity to re-evaluate our priorities and align our actions with our values and

aspirations. It helps us gain clarity on our next steps and make informed decisions moving forward.

Section 3: Cultivating Lifelong Learning Habits

Lifelong learning is the continuous process of acquiring knowledge skills and insights throughout our lives. Cultivating lifelong learning habits is crucial for personal growth and adaptability in an ever-changing world. Here are some effective strategies for fostering lifelong learning:

1. Curiosity: Maintain a sense of curiosity and a thirst for knowledge. Ask questions seek answers and explore various subjects of interest.

2. Reading: Develop a habit of reading regularly. Books articles and other written materials broaden our horizons and expose us to new ideas.

3. Networking: Engage with diverse individuals and communities to gain different perspectives and learn from a wide range of experiences.

4. Embrace challenges: Embrace challenges as opportunities for learning and growth. Step out of your comfort zone and take on new tasks that push you to acquire new skills.

5. Reflect and review: Take time to reflect on what you have learned review your progress and identify areas where you can continue to grow and develop.

By celebrating milestones reflecting on progress and cultivating lifelong learning habits we can experience personal and professional growth. These practices contribute to our overall success well-being and satisfaction with life. Embrace these habits and continue to grow throughout your journey.

Personal growth tip

Here are 100 personal growth tips for your continued growth and development:

1. Set meaningful goals for yourself.
   2. Develop a positive mindset and focus on gratitude.
   3. Take responsibility for your actions decisions and outcomes.
   4. Invest in continuous learning and personal development.
   5. Surround yourself with positive and supportive people.
   6. Practice self-compassion and self-care.
   7. Cultivate healthy habits like exercise proper nutrition and adequate sleep.
   8. Embrace change and be open to new experiences.
   9. Practice regular reflection and self-assessment.
   10. Develop effective time management skills.
   11. Improve your communication skills.
   12. Learn to listen actively and empathetically.
   13. Practice mindfulness and meditation to reduce stress and increase self-awareness.
   14. Embrace failure as an opportunity to learn and grow.
   15. Seek feedback and be open to constructive criticism.
   16. Develop your emotional intelligence and self-awareness.

17. Cultivate resilience to overcome challenges and setbacks.

18. Set healthy boundaries in your personal and professional life.

19. Practice assertiveness to effectively communicate your needs and desires.

20. Foster a growth mindset that embraces learning and continuous improvement.

21. Develop your problem-solving and decision-making skills.

22. Build a strong support network of mentors and role models.

23. Develop your leadership skills regardless of your position.

24. Take calculated risks to push yourself outside of your comfort zone.

25. Practice patience and perseverance in pursuing your goals.

26. Nurture and maintain healthy relationships with family and friends.

27. Develop your emotional regulation skills to manage stress and emotions effectively.

28. Engage in activities that bring you joy and fulfillment.

29. Cultivate a sense of purpose and meaning in your life.

30. Foster a sense of gratitude and appreciation for the present moment.

31. Stay curious and never stop learning.

32. Practice effective decision-making by considering the long-term consequences.

33. Learn to let go of negative emotions and forgive yourself and others.

34. Practice empathy and compassion towards yourself and others.

35. Cultivate a growth mindset by embracing challenges and failures as opportunities for learning.

36. Seek opportunities for personal and professional growth through workshops courses and conferences.

37. Read books that inspire and challenge your perspectives.

38. Develop a daily routine that includes self-care activities.

39. Engage in hobbies and activities that bring you joy and relaxation.

40. Set boundaries and prioritize your self-care needs.

41. Learn to say no when necessary to avoid overwhelm.

42. Practice active listening in your interactions with others.

43. Seek out diverse perspectives and experiences.

44. Engage in constructive self-talk and positive affirmations.

45. Practice gratitude journaling to cultivate a positive mindset.

46. Develop effective stress management techniques such as deep breathing or exercise.

47. Take breaks and recharge when needed to avoid burnout.

48. Seek opportunities for personal and professional networking.

49. Develop your problem-solving skills through puzzles and brain-teasers.

50. Practice visualization techniques to manifest your goals and desires.

51. Embrace challenges as opportunities for growth and learning.

52. Develop your creativity through activities like painting writing or playing an instrument.

53. Seek feedback from trusted mentors or coaches to gain new perspectives.

54. Celebrate your successes no matter how small.

55. Prioritize your physical health by making regular exercise a part of your routine.

56. Establish a consistent sleep schedule to promote overall well-being.

57. Engage in activities that foster self-expression and self-discovery.

58. Foster a growth mindset by reframing failures as learning opportunities.

59. Develop your financial literacy and practice responsible financial management.

60. Volunteer or engage in acts of kindness to give back to your community.

61. Develop your problem-solving skills by tackling puzzles or brain teasers.

62. Learn to effectively manage conflicts and disagreements.

63. Take ownership of your personal and professional growth by seeking out resources and opportunities.

64. Practice journaling to increase self-reflection and self-awareness.

65. Set aside dedicated time for relaxation and self-care.

66. Seek out new experiences and challenges to expand your comfort zone.

67. Set boundaries and practice saying "no" to things that don't align with your values or goals.

68. Cultivate a growth mindset by embracing challenges and failures as opportunities for learning.

69. Seek opportunities for personal and professional growth through workshops courses and conferences.

70. Develop a growth mindset by believing in your ability to learn and improve.

71. Actively seek feedback from mentors and peers to foster personal growth.

72. Practice mindfulness to increase self-awareness and

reduce stress.

73. Foster a positive body image and practice self-acceptance.

74. Surround yourself with positive and supportive people who inspire and motivate you.

75. Develop your emotional intelligence to improve your relationships and communication skills.

76. Engage in regular physical activity to improve both your physical and mental well-being.

77. Seek opportunities to step outside of your comfort zone and take on new challenges.

78. Practice gratitude by regularly acknowledging and appreciating the good things in your life.

79. Set clear boundaries to protect your physical emotional and mental well-being.

80. Embrace failure as a stepping stone to success and learn from your mistakes.

81. Cultivate a growth mindset by viewing setbacks as opportunities for growth and improvement.

82. Regularly assess your goals and make adjustments as needed.

83. Prioritize self-care activities that nourish your mind body and soul.

84. Engage in regular self-reflection to gain insights into your strengths weaknesses and areas for growth.

85. Take time to disconnect from technology and spend quality time in nature.

86. Develop effective problem-solving skills by breaking down complex challenges into manageable steps.

87. Seek out mentors and role models who can offer guidance and support in your personal growth journey.

88. Practice effective communication skills including active

listening and clear expression of thoughts and feelings.

89. Set aside time for hobbies and activities that bring you joy and fulfillment.

90. Foster a growth mindset by embracing challenges and reframing failures as opportunities for learning.

91. Practice time management techniques to maximize productivity and minimize distractions.

92. Cultivate self-compassion by treating yourself with kindness and understanding.

93. Foster a sense of curiosity by seeking out new knowledge and experiences.

94. Embrace self-reflection as a tool for personal growth and development.

95. Practice effective stress management techniques such as deep breathing meditation or engaging in hobbies.

96. Build strong and meaningful relationships by investing time and effort into fostering connections with others.

97. Seek out opportunities to learn from different perspectives and cultures.

98. Set aside time for personal reflection and goal-setting.

99. Embrace the power of positive affirmations and visualization techniques.

100. Celebrate your progress and milestones along your personal growth journey.

Remember personal growth is a lifelong process so be patient and kind to yourself as you implement these tips.

Skill development tips

100 skill development tips to help you enhance your abilities and achieve your goals:

Personal Growth and Development:

1. Set clear goals: Define specific, measurable, achievable, relevant, and time-bound (SMART) goals.
2. Embrace lifelong learning: Commit to continuous self-improvement and acquiring new knowledge.
3. Practice self-awareness: Reflect on your strengths, weaknesses, and areas for improvement.
4. Develop a growth mindset: Believe in your ability to learn and adapt to new challenges.
5. Manage your time: Prioritize tasks, set deadlines, and avoid multitasking.
6. Master effective communication: Improve your verbal, nonverbal, and written communication skills.
7. Cultivate emotional intelligence: Understand and manage your own emotions while empathizing with others.
8. Enhance your critical thinking: Analyze situations objectively and make informed decisions.

9. Practice mindfulness: Develop the ability to stay present and focused on the task at hand.
10. Learn stress management techniques: Handle pressure and setbacks with resilience.
11. Prioritize self-care: Maintain a healthy balance between work, rest, and play.
12. Foster adaptability: Embrace change and develop the ability to thrive in various environments.
13. Build self-confidence: Believe in your abilities and project a positive self-image.
14. Cultivate a strong work ethic: Demonstrate dedication, discipline, and commitment in your endeavors.
15. Develop problem-solving skills: Find creative solutions to challenges that arise.

Professional Skills:

16. Master time management: Allocate time effectively to tasks and projects.

17. Develop organizational skills: Create systems to manage information, tasks, and resources.

18. Hone your leadership abilities: Inspire, motivate, and guide individuals or teams.

19. Improve your decision-making: Make well-informed choices based on data and analysis.

20. Develop negotiation skills: Find win-win solutions and manage conflicts effectively.

21. Excel in public speaking: Communicate confidently and engage audiences.

22. Enhance your networking skills: Build and maintain

valuable professional relationships.

23. Learn project management: Plan, execute, and complete tasks within scope, time, and budget.

24. Become tech-savvy: Stay updated with relevant technology and tools in your field.

25. Develop financial literacy: Understand basic financial concepts and manage your finances.

26. Master data analysis: Interpret and draw insights from data to inform decisions.

27. Cultivate research skills: Gather, evaluate, and synthesize information effectively.

28. Improve your writing skills: Express ideas clearly and persuasively in writing.

29. Develop sales and marketing skills: Promote products or ideas effectively to target audiences.

30. Build customer service skills: Provide exceptional support and assistance to clients.

Creativity and Innovation:

31. Practice brainstorming: Generate a variety of ideas without judgment.

32. Embrace curiosity: Explore new concepts and seek to understand different perspectives.

33. Foster a creative environment: Surround yourself with inspiration and diverse stimuli.

34. Experiment with different approaches: Test new methods and strategies.

35. Combine unrelated ideas: Fuse concepts from different domains to create novel solutions.

36. Practice lateral thinking: Solve problems through uncon-

ventional and indirect methods.

37. Seek feedback: Gather input from others to refine and improve your ideas.

38. Develop storytelling skills: Convey information and concepts through compelling narratives.

39. Create a vision board: Visualize your goals and aspirations to spark creativity.

40. Learn from failures: Analyze mistakes and setbacks to uncover valuable insights.

Communication Skills:

41. Active listening: Pay close attention and show empathy when others speak.

42. Practice nonverbal communication: Use gestures, facial expressions, and body language effectively.

43. Develop empathy: Understand and share the feelings of others to enhance relationships.

44. Improve your negotiation skills: Find common ground and reach mutually beneficial agreements.

45. Enhance your persuasive skills: Present arguments and ideas in a compelling manner.

46. Learn cross-cultural communication: Adapt your communication style to different cultures.

47. Develop conflict resolution skills: Manage disagreements constructively and find solutions.

48. Use visual aids: Create and utilize visual tools to enhance your communication.

49. Master storytelling: Craft engaging narratives to convey messages effectively.

50. Practice concise communication: Express ideas clearly

and succinctly.

Technical and Practical Skills:

51. Learn coding and programming: Develop skills in languages relevant to your field.

52. Excel in data analysis: Use software and tools to analyze and interpret data.

53. Develop graphic design skills: Create visually appealing and impactful designs.

54. Learn video editing: Edit and produce high-quality videos for various purposes.

55. Master a foreign language: Enhance your ability to communicate with a wider audience.

56. Develop culinary skills: Learn to prepare diverse and delicious dishes.

57. Practice woodworking: Create functional and aesthetic items from wood.

58. Learn basic car maintenance: Perform routine tasks to keep your vehicle in good condition.

59. Develop gardening skills: Cultivate plants, flowers, or vegetables.

60. Master DIY home repairs: Tackle basic household fixes and improvements.

Physical and Health-Related Skills:

61. Develop a fitness routine: Exercise regularly to maintain physical health.

62. Learn yoga or meditation: Practice techniques to enhance mental and emotional well-being.

63. Develop cooking skills: Prepare nutritious meals for yourself and others.

64. Master a sport: Improve your skills in a chosen athletic activity.

65. Learn first aid and CPR: Acquire life-saving skills for emergencies.

66. Practice mindfulness: Cultivate awareness and presence in everyday activities.

67. Develop flexibility: Engage in stretching and mobility exercises.

68. Learn self-defense: Acquire techniques to protect yourself in challenging situations.

69. Master a dance style: Improve coordination and expressiveness through dance.

70. Develop swimming skills: Learn to swim and improve water safety.

Artistic and Creative Skills:

71. Learn to play a musical instrument: Acquire proficiency in playing music.

72. Develop painting or drawing skills: Express yourself through visual art forms.

73. Learn photography: Capture compelling images and moments.

74. Practice creative writing: Write stories, poems, or essays to express your ideas.

75. Master acting or theater: Enhance your expressive and performance abilities.

76. Develop sculpting skills: Create three-dimensional art using various materials.

77. Learn calligraphy: Practice the art of beautiful handwriting.

78. Practice digital art: Create visual art using digital tools and software.

79. Develop singing skills: Improve your vocal range and technique.

80. Learn ceramics: Create functional and decorative items from clay.

Financial Skills:

81. Budgeting and financial planning: Manage your finances effectively and save money.

82. Learn about investing: Understand different investment options and strategies.

83. Develop stock market knowledge: Learn how to analyze and trade stocks.

84. Improve your credit management: Build and maintain a strong credit history.

85. Learn about real estate: Understand property investments and transactions.

86. Practice frugality: Make wise spending choices and live within your means.

87. Develop entrepreneurship skills: Start and manage a small business or venture.

88. Learn about taxes: Understand tax laws and how to file your taxes.

89. Master personal finance: Make informed decisions about loans, mortgages, and retirement planning.

90. Develop financial literacy: Understand economic concepts and global financial trends.

Technology and Digital Skills:

91. Learn cloud computing: Familiarize yourself with cloud platforms and services.

92. Develop cybersecurity skills:Enhance your ability to protect digital assets and data.

93. Learn about artificial intelligence: Understand AI concepts and applications.

94. Master social media marketing: Utilize social platforms for business or personal branding.

95. Develop website development skills: Create and maintain websites using coding or CMS platforms.

96. Learn about blockchain technology: Understand the fundamentals of decentralized systems.

97. Practice video game design: Create and develop your own video game concepts.

98. Develop mobile app development skills: Create applications for smartphones and tablets.

99. Learn about digital marketing: Enhance your skills in online advertising and promotion.

100. Master data science: Analyze and interpret large datasets to derive meaningful insights.

www.ingramcontent.com/pod-product-compliance
Lightning Source LLC
Chambersburg PA
CBHW072337290526
45794CB00002B/916